PIRATES!

Liz Miles

Illustrated by Leo Hartas

Horus Editions

Author: Liz Miles
Illustrations: Leo Hartas
Design: Duck Egg Blue

ISBN 978-1-899762-91-0

Copyright © 2008 Horus Editions

First published 2008

Published by Horus Editions
an imprint of
Award Publications Limited,
The Old Riding School,
The Welbeck Estate, Worksop,
Nottinghamshire, S80 3LR

10 9 8 7 6 5 4 3 2 1
20 19 18 17 16 15 14 13 12 10 11 10 09 08

Printed in China

Contents

The Gruesome Truth!

You really wouldn't want to meet a real-life pirate. The chances are you wouldn't escape from such an encounter alive, because pirates were notorious for their cut-throat attacks on ships, stealing their valuable cargoes and murdering the passengers and crew.

Pirates have been a menace to sailing ships across the oceans and around coasts since ancient times. They have gone by many names: buccaneers, corsairs, sea rovers, sea beggars, freebooters, filibusters and pickaroons.

Piracy was at its worst during the years when the Spanish and Portuguese brought home fabulous cargoes of gold from newly-conquered Central and South America. Their heavily-laden galleons were irresistible targets. Not surprisingly, most of the pirates that appear in storybooks and films are from these dangerous times.

How do you imagine a pirate should look? A fierce-looking man with a beard, a wooden leg, and a parrot on his shoulder? Or perhaps a handsome rogue like Captain Jack Sparrow from the film *Pirates of the Caribbean?* Does this picture match your idea of the pirate world?

Stolen wig – fashionable in the 18th century

Eye patch covering a horrible wound

Scabby skin, rotten teeth and bad breath caused by scurvy

Notorious Pirates from Stories and Films

Adventure stories involving pirates have always been popular. The most famous is Robert Louis Stevenson's *Treasure Island*, published in 1883. It set the pattern for future pirate stories.

Here are a few well-known pirate characters. You can look them up on the Internet or at your library if you want to know more about them:

- Long John Silver, Captain Flint (from the novel *Treasure Island*)
- Buggy the Clown (from a Japanese animation, *One Piece*)
- Captain Pugwash (John Ryan's character featured in comics, books and animations)
- Redbeard (Belgian comics)
- Captain Jack Sparrow (from the film, *Pirates of the Caribbean*)
- Captain Hook (J.M. Barrie's novel, *Peter Pan and Wendy*)

Captain Hook

Skull and crossbones – the emblem on a pirate flag, known as the Jolly Roger

Parrot – caught in the Americas and traded in Europe

Why be a pirate?

In the 'Golden Age of Piracy' (from about 1690–1725) those who became pirates did so in the hope that they could get rich quickly. Many seamen from England and America took to piracy after deserting from the Navy. Some, such as doctors and soldiers, were already wealthy when they joined a pirate ship. They may have been running from the law, or were just greedy.

Eustace the Monk

Eustace the Monk gave up life as a church cleric for the dangerous life of piracy. He wasn't fussy who he worked for and sold his pirate services to the English and then the French. Eustace's adventures ended dramatically after the English captured him and chopped off his head.

Musket

Gold earring – kept to pay for a pirate's own burial

Fine clothes, stolen of course

Cutlass – an ideal weapon for cutting off heads

Old metal hook, in place of a hand lopped off in battle

Wooden leg, or 'peg leg'

Knife – an all-round useful weapon, especially for cutting throats or food

Treasure (also called loot or booty) – any cargo worth stealing

Doubloons – Spanish gold

Early Pirates

In the 'civilised' days of Ancient Greece and the Roman Empire, uncivilised pirates used to prey on the rich cargo vessels that regularly sailed across the Mediterranean Sea. A slow, single-sail merchant ship was soon overtaken by a speedy pirate galley, powered by a team of strong oarsmen.

Around 500BC, pirates lurked in bays around the Greek islands in the Aegean Sea, waiting for a ship full of silver, copper or amber to pass by.

Ancient Rome's pirates were so bold they even kidnapped the young Julius Caesar in 75BC. He was kept on a tiny island for five weeks until a ransom was paid. But Caesar soon got his own back – a few months after his release, the pirates were found and crucified.

Single mainsail

Pirates outnumbered the soldiers and crew on a cargo ship

Ramming a cargo ship was an effective method of attack

In spite of their training, Roman soldiers were no match for the savage pirates

Deep-bottomed, heavy cargo ships were slow and cumbersome

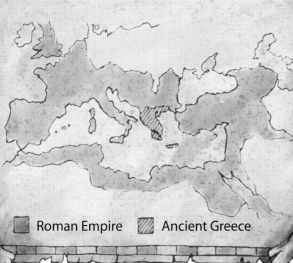

The Ancient Greek and Roman Worlds

Roman Empire   Ancient Greece

Robbing Romans

In 67BC, Pompey the Great (a Roman general) led a fleet of ships to put an end to pirates who were stealing vast amounts of precious grain. The Roman army was sent out as well, to destroy the pirates' base in Cilicia. However, in spite of both these efforts, pirates soon reappeared in Mediterranean waters.

A pirate galley in the days of the Roman Empire

Because of their shallow bottoms, galleys were easy to steer

Sails and oarsmen made the ship move fast

Painted eyes were for good luck

Violent Vikings

Years later, in the 9th century, and up in the North Sea, the Vikings of Scandinavia terrified people with their piracy. They travelled swiftly in longboats carrying as many as fifty warriors, all eager to get their hands on anything they could find. Vikings became infamous for their pillaging (violent theft) along the British coast.

Steering oar

Cold~blooded Corsairs

From about 1500 to 1800, corsairs were paid by warring Christian Crusaders and Muslims to destroy each other's ships in and around the Mediterranean Sea. Barbary corsairs sailed in galleys armed with small cannons. They usually just rammed enemy Christian ships, then jumped aboard for a fight to the death with swords, for which they were notorious. Christian corsairs felt safer behind a cannon.

Corsairs generally stole people, not treasure. Barbary corsairs could demand a high ransom if they captured a wealthy knight. Prisoners were brutally treated and most were kept to be sold as slaves, or used to row the galleys. Up to 90 might be chained together below deck and forced to row until they died.

Sometimes a knight captained a Christian ship

Barbary corsairs had the finest swords and daggers in the world

Some Christian corsairs were lucky enough to have muskets

The 'Barbarossa Brothers'

Aruj and Kheir-ed-din were Muslim brothers and the most feared of Barbary corsairs. Their nickname comes from their red beards (*barba rossa* is Latin for 'red beard'). Among their many pirate 'successes' was the cunning capture of ships belonging to the Pope. By 1510, at the age of about 36, Aruj was probably the richest man in the Mediterranean.

Christians called the Muslim corsairs 'barbarians'

Crusading Knights

From about 1100AD, Christian knights went on Crusades to recapture the Holy Land from the ruling Muslims. A group of wealthy Crusaders, called the Knights of Malta, settled on the island of Malta in the Mediterranean Sea. They built a large fleet and employed Christian corsairs to lead the fight against the Barbary corsairs.

Knight of Malta

Dragut Rais – a cruel leader of Barbary corsairs. If his prisoners were too ill or old to be ransomed or used as slaves, he had them killed

Barbary corsairs used well-trained, professional soldiers called Janissaries to do most of the fighting

GRUESOME TRUTH!

Dragut Rais asked a sailor for a bunch of grapes. When the sailor brought him a bunch with a broken stalk, he ordered the sailor to be burnt to death.

Barbary corsairs thought of themselves as law-abiding privateers

Licensed to Plunder ~ the Privateers

The waves of treasure-laden Spanish ships crossing the Atlantic Ocean, on their way home from their South and Central American conquests (the Spanish Main) caught the greedy eyes of the kings and queens of France and England, who were just as keen to share this bounty as the pirates. They gave a special licence, known as a 'letter of marque', to privately-owned ships, employing them to attack enemy (Spanish) vessels in return for half their booty. Some of these privateers took advantage of this and happily accosted any ship that happened to be passing.

Sir Francis Drake's 'treasure map'

Sir Francis Drake (c. 1540–1596) is something of a hero, much admired today for sailing round the world and defeating the Spanish Armada. But Drake was Queen Elizabeth I's favourite privateer, a pirate and pilferer of Spanish ships, and said to have brought her treasure worth £200,000 (millions in today's money) from his successes. Elizabeth called him 'her pirate'. The Spanish had a different view, and called Drake *El Draque* – the Dragon.

The map (right) shows some of the major events during Drake's privateering days.

Knighthood

After his very successful world voyage, Drake returned to England in 1580 with fabulous riches, including 26 tonnes of Spanish gold, silver, coins and gems. For his service to the realm, Drake was given a knighthood by the Queen on the deck of the *Golden Hind* in 1581.

Arise, Sir Pirate! ... Oops! I mean, arise, Sir Francis!

1586

In April, Drake's men raided the town of San Augustin (in the part of North America we now call Florida), looting and burning it to the ground. With this kind of heavy-handed piracy Drake certainly lived up to his draconian name.

1568

Early on in Drake's career at sea, he had a nasty experience during a trading voyage when his fleet was attacked in a Spanish port in Mexico, and Drake watched as a friend's vessel was destroyed by a Spanish fire-ship.

1579 March

While sailing across the Pacific Ocean, Drake seized a treasure ship, the *Nuestra Señora de la Concepción*, which happened to belong to the King of Spain himself. It took more than 6 days to move its cargo of gold and silver into Drake's ship.

1578

The captain of a Spanish treasure ship, anchored at Valparaiso, invited Drake and his men to dinner, believing them to be Spanish! Once aboard, Drake locked up his horrified hosts and made off with a thousand jars of wine and four leather chests packed with gold.

1586

Drake had set off the year before with a fleet of 29 ships to take or destroy Spanish lands and vessels. After looting and destroying most of the Spanish town of Santo Domingo in 1586, he demanded a ransom of 25,000 ducats, saying, "Pay or else I'll burn the rest!"

1577

Drake began his three-year life of piracy, journeying around the world in a ship called the *Pelican* (later renamed the *Golden Hind*).

1573

This time, when Drake and his men ambushed a mule train taking treasure to Nombre de Dios, the escort of 50 Spanish guards simply ran away. The loot was worth about £40,000 (£4 million in today's money).

1572

Drake attacked the Spanish city of Nombre de Dios, Panama, but failed to steal its treasure. He had to be carried back to his ship after being shot in the leg with a musket ball.

N

W

E

S

Brutal Buccaneers

Once King James of England withdrew all 'letters of marque' in 1603, the Caribbean faced a new, deadlier kind of pirate – the buccaneers. Although now infamous for both their brutality and lawlessness, the original buccaneers were fairly peaceful people living on the islands of Cuba, Jamaica and Hispaniola (now Haiti and the Dominican Republic). Their name comes from the 'boucans' (smokehouses) they used to barbecue the meat they traded with passing ships.

When the Spanish tried to drive the buccaneers from the islands, they formed a brotherhood – the Brethren of the Coast – and fought back. It wasn't long before self-defence turned into hostile attacks on Spanish ships and settlements. Their successes attracted seedier, greedier types, such as outlaws and convicts, who joined the brotherhood in the hope of getting a share of the Spanish riches.

Pirate Insurance Policy

The Buccaneer Brethren had a table of compensation for any serious wounds they might receive at sea.

100 pieces of eight for an eye

600 pieces of eight for a right hand (sword-holding hand)

500 pieces of eight for a left arm

500 pieces of eight for a right leg

100 pieces of eight for a finger

400 pieces of eight for a left leg

Sneak attacks were best done in dull light, such as moonlight.

Loot was divided among the crew; the captain got five times more than a crewman

An eye-patch, covering an injury, was worn like a badge of honour

Bloodthirsty Tyrants

The buccaneers were notoriously cruel. Roche Brasiliano was a brutal drunkard who once roasted two Spanish farmers alive over a fire. The French buccaneer, François L'Ollonais, tortured his prisoners by chopping them up, bits at a time. The more famous Welshman, Sir Henry Morgan, was given a knighthood for his attacks on Spanish settlements. In one town on Hispaniola, he locked all the Spanish inhabitants in the churches and left them to starve to death.

Roche Brasiliano   François L'Ollonais   Sir Henry Morgan

Buccaneers chose their captain; if he wasn't up to scratch, they simply chose another

The buccaneers invented the cutlass – it was similar to the large knives they used to cut meat

Buccaneers wore clothes made of uncured animal hides

A small boat could more easily dodge cannon fire than a large ship

A dugout canoe (or *piragua*) was ideal for sneaking up on ships

GRUESOME TRUTH!

To discover the whereabouts of hidden treasure, buccaneers tied and stretched their victims on a rack, until they talked.

Grand Galleons and Sneaky Sloops

Homeward-bound Spanish galleons, stuffed with treasure, were at the top of every pirate's 'must have' list. These grand, stately wooden sailing ships, although impressive, were slow and difficult to steer with their heavy cargoes, so they were easy prey for the pirates.

The Spanish soon realised that there was greater safety in numbers, so convoys of up to a hundred vessels would set sail together, sometimes escorted by heavily-armed warships. The warships often kept well behind, ready to take any approaching pirate ship by surprise.

'Crow's nest', where a lookout kept watch for danger, including pirates

Each deck had a different name: poop deck, quarterdeck orlop deck, weather deck and main deck – this is the fo'c's'le (forecastle)

Up to 30 heavy cannons lined each side

Treasure was locked away in chests on the lower decks

Soldiers guarded the cargo

Hull

Main mast

A galleon carried a crew of about 200 men

Captain's cabin

Light cannons at the stern

The Pirate Ships

Pirates chased their prey in all kinds of vessels. Generally, small was best. Smaller ships had a low profile on the water, and were swift and easy to steer, so ideal for slipping out of hidden bays, to take their targets by surprise. For pirates in the 1600s, sloops (small warships) were their preferred choice, although most had to make do with what they could steal. Sloops had a good-sized hold for cargo, but because of their shallow draught, they could sail into shallow coastal waters, and hide in sheltered bays.

Privateers, on the other hand, might have a whole fleet of prizes, including schooners, sloops, frigates and even galleons.

A pirate sloop usually had only 6 light cannons, or fewer

GRUESOME TRUTH!

When Inca emperor Atahualpa was captured by Spanish invaders, he offered a room full of gold in exchange for his release. The Spanish took the gold, then killed Atahualpa.

Pirates of the Caribbean

Blackbeard, Bonnet and Bart

Early in his career as a pirate, Blackbeard soon impressed his captain with his fierce cruelty. It is said that instead of asking for a prisoner's diamond ring, he just cut off the ringed finger and put both ring and finger in his pocket! Blackbeard acquired his own ship in 1717 (the *Queen Anne's Revenge*). In 1718, the Royal Navy brought an end to his evil ways, but it took 20 cutlass wounds and 5 gunshots to kill the powerful pirate.

Unlike Blackbeard, Stede Bonnet was a gentleman. Blackbeard laughed at Bonnet when he first saw the plump, clean-shaven dandy. The retired army major was a bungler at sea and a hopeless pirate, so Blackbeard soon took command of Bonnet and his ship.

Black Bart was a brilliant seaman and a better pirate than Blackbeard. No more than a mate on a slave ship, he jumped at the chance of becoming a captain of a pirate ship in 1719.

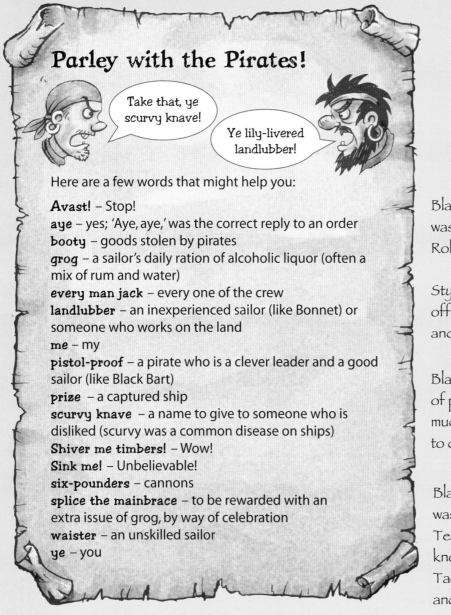

Black Bart (c. 1682–1722) plundered as least 400 ships during his pirate years

Black Bart's real name was Captain Bartholomew Roberts

Stylish clothes showed off Bart's new-found power and wealth as a pirate

Black Bart disapproved of pirates who drank too much liquor; he preferred to drink tea and stay sober

Blackbeard's real name was probably Edward Teach – but he was also known as Drummond, Tach, Thatch, Tatch and Tash

Parley with the Pirates!

Take that, ye scurvy knave!

Ye lily-livered landlubber!

Here are a few words that might help you:

Avast! – Stop!
aye – yes; 'Aye, aye,' was the correct reply to an order
booty – goods stolen by pirates
grog – a sailor's daily ration of alcoholic liquor (often a mix of rum and water)
every man jack – every one of the crew
landlubber – an inexperienced sailor (like Bonnet) or someone who works on the land
me – my
pistol-proof – a pirate who is a clever leader and a good sailor (like Black Bart)
prize – a captured ship
scurvy knave – a name to give to someone who is disliked (scurvy was a common disease on ships)
Shiver me timbers! – Wow!
Sink me! – Unbelievable!
six-pounders – cannons
splice the mainbrace – to be rewarded with an extra issue of grog, by way of celebration
waister – an unskilled sailor
ye – you

Faced with two sharp-edged cutlasses, many victims chose to surrender

Stede Bonnet was well-educated and came from a wealthy family

Bonnet (c. 1688–1718) dressed like a gentleman and wore a powdered wig

A pirate's paradise

In the early 17th century, most of the world's five thousand pirates were plundering ships and coastal settlements in the Caribbean Sea. Spanish ships carrying slaves, treasures and sugar were easy prey to the pirate ships that hid in bays around the islands.

Blackbeard also terrorised the coasts of Carolina and Virginia, especially the plantations of the early English settlers. In 1718, he blockaded the whole harbour at the port of Charleston. He even took a council member and his son prisoner and only released them in exchange for a chest full of medicines.

Blackbeard kept six pistols in his baldric (belt)

For battle, Blackbeard decked his costume out with slow-burning fuses – a terrifying sight

NORTH AMERICA

VIRGINIA
CAROLINA
Charleston
Blackbeard died here

N
W   E
S

CARIBBEAN SEA

SOUTH AMERICA

Women Pirates

It was a general rule at sea that no women were allowed on board ship. They were considered bad-luck by the crew, and captains thought them bad for discipline. But there were some women who managed to join a ship by dressing and behaving like men. Anne Bonny and Mary Read were the most famous.

Born in Ireland, Anne Bonny began a pirate's life in the sunny Bahamas when she married pirate James Bonny. Later, she left him for another pirate, Calico Jack Rackham (called 'Calico' because of the fancy calico trousers he wore). They were joined by Mary Read. Both Anne and Mary were tough and courageous, and they became the best of buddies.

In 1720, a British navy sloop attacked Jack's ship. Anne and Mary were the only crew members sober enough to fight, but in spite of their brave efforts, they were all taken prisoner. Anne and Mary both escaped hanging because they were pregnant!

Anne Bonny and Calico Jack sailed together for more than three years

As Calico Jack went to the gallows, Anne angrily said: "Had you fought like a man, you need not have been hanged like a dog."

Flintlock pistol

Pirates used heavy axes as tools and weapons

Mary Read, born in England, dressed as a man to join the army when she was a teenager

Mary was on her way to her new army posting when Calico Jack captured the ship she was on

A loose-fitting jacket and shirt disguised Mary's female figure

After an argument with another pirate, Mary challenged him to a cutlass duel and won

A Runaway Princess

One of the first powerful female pirates was Alvilda, Princess of Gotland (now Sweden). She ran away from home to become a pirate when her parents tried to make her marry Alf, the Prince of Denmark.

She and her all-female crew terrorised ships and villages along the Baltic Sea coast, until their ship was eventually captured by a fleet sent out by the King of Denmark, captained by none other than Alf – the prince she had refused to marry.

Gang Leader

Sadie 'the Goat' was leader of a New York group of gangsters in the 1860s. She and her gang stole a sloop, raised the Jolly Roger and raided ships and houses along the Hudson River. She was particularly fond of kidnapping wealthy citizens and demanding ransoms. Her nickname comes from her habit of head-butting victims in the stomach!

Pirates at Work and Play

Life on board a pirate ship could be exciting, dangerous, frightening and, sometimes, very boring. The biggest buzz came with the chase and capture of a treasure ship. But there were times when there was little to do except routine work to keep the ship afloat and the crew alive. There were often repairs to be done to the ship, especially after a battle or a storm.

Pirates passed their free time in numerous ways. As well as getting drunk they played card games, sang and danced to a fiddle or a squeezebox and made up pantomime trials. The 'trials' involved acting out a mock trial in which each pirate took a role, such as a judge, a lawyer, and even a hangman.

Sailing the ship required strong muscles and stamina. Crew members worked together, forever climbing up and down rigging, and pulling at ropes and sails to keep up the speed and to stay on course.

Upper decks were swabbed with a mix of seawater and vinegar, while lower decks were fumigated to rid them of vermin, by burning pitch or brimstone.

The ship's carpenter was responsible for repairs to any part of the wooden ship damaged in battles or storms.

Not all pirate ships carried a surgeon or doctor. Most made do with anyone who had carpentry skills! Battle wounds were the worst: shattered legs and arms were sawn off, splinters and shot removed, and wounds sewn up. Instruments were limited to a few knives, tiny spoons, a needle, some thread, and a saw.

Nearly all the food and liquid stored on board were kept in barrels, so a cooper (barrel-maker) was a handy man to have about.

Rigging and sails had to be kept in good condition. Rope-work was skilled, involving special terms and tools. To splice (join two ropes), a fid (pointed instrument) was used to first separate the ropes' strands.

A damp blanket on the forecastle (fo'c's'le) deck was all a common pirate had for a bed.

Dancing a jig lifted the pirates' spirits. During a battle, musicians sometimes played ominous notes on drums and trumpets to demoralise the enemy.

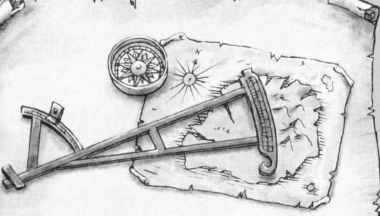

Navigation

Every ship needed a good navigator if its crew were to find their quarry or their home base again. The job involved using a compass to estimate how far west or east the ship had sailed (longitude) and a cross-staff or backstaff to measure how far north or south the ship was (latitude).

Stolen charts (maps) of newly-discovered lands helped the navigator to work out how best to find the common routes followed by treasure ships.

GRUESOME TRUTH!

There were no anaesthetics. Shipmates requiring surgery just had to get drunk enough to feel less of the pain.

Food and Vermin

Living on board a wooden sailing ship was not pleasant, and there were lots of rather nasty things in a pirate's life. Poor nutrition and a dangerous lifestyle meant that few could escape disease, sickness or injury.

Food was basic and seldom fresh. Preserved meats were over-salty, dry and tough. Fresh meat was usually limited to any fish caught from the ship. Turtles were sometimes captured on Caribbean coasts and kept alive in the hold until needed. Hens were also kept alive, both for their meat and for their 'cackle-fruit' (eggs). Towards the end of a long voyage, baked ships' biscuits – called 'hardtack' because they were so tough to bite – were usually the only alternative to starvation.

Fresh water soon went stale, so beer was the common drink for all mariners. Brandy was a favourite with the pirates, although grog (rum and water) was happily knocked back, too.

Food was prepared in the galley (ship's kitchen)

Some pirates ate from pewter plates

Sickness ~ the Feverish Facts

- Typhus and typhoid fever could wipe out half a ship's crew on a single voyage.

- Scurvy (bleeding gums, black teeth, blotchy skin) was caused by the lack of vitamin C in a pirate's diet of meat and biscuits.

- The wet conditions on a wooden ship caused cramps and colds.

- A bite from an infected mosquito could lead to malaria or yellow fever (serious tropical diseases).

- As there were no proper toilets and little water to wash in, bacteria spread rapidly through the ship's crew, with serious, even deadly, results.

Pirates, sometimes called sea wolves, probably had as few table manners as animals

Stolen forks were used occasionally, but knives, spoons and fingers were the most common 'cutlery'

Nasty Creatures

Rats spread disease on ships and could even sink a ship by gnawing holes in the wooden hull. Along with cockroaches and beetles, hundreds of rats lived amongst the wet rubbish in the bottom (bilge) of a ship. Unfortunate crew members were sent down to this stinking place to find and kill the pests.

Many pirates died of scurvy, until – in 1747 – James Lind proved that the disease could be prevented by eating citrus fruit regularly

Earthenware bottles of beer

'Hardtack' biscuits were often full of maggots by the time they were eaten

In desperation, some famished buccaneers ate their coat, satchel or belt leather – after slicing, soaking, beating, and grilling it!

Vermin appeared wherever there was food. Rats were often eaten if food was scarce

Action!

As soon as their quarry was sighted by the lookout, the pirates took a vote on whether to attack. If the result was 'yes', a cannon was fired and the Jolly Roger raised. Horrific tales of pirates' cruelty made many sailors surrender at first sight of the flag. But if they chose to put up a fight, the pirates were prepared.

To stop any return cannon fire the pirates tried to shoot anyone trying to light a fuse on the enemy ship. Within minutes, the speedy pirate ship was ramming its prey. After a quick turn, it then came alongside, and the pirates threw grappling irons and ropes across. Soon they were swinging themselves onto the enemy deck. A savage, noisy fight to the death followed. Because there were many more men on a pirate ship than sailors on a merchant ship, the battle was usually short.

Pirates hacked open locked doors and hatches to get at the booty

Passengers on the cargo ship had to fight for their lives

Now me-hearty, where's the treasure?

Sneaky Tricks

At night, pirates sometimes crept on board their victims' ship while it was in port and the crew were asleep. Pirates might also disguise their ship as a harmless merchant vessel. They camouflaged the gunports and flew a friendly flag. Most of the pirates hid below deck until their prize was within firing range. Then the pirates revealed their ship's true identity by raising the Jolly Roger or firing a shot over the other ship's bow.

Once fired, a pistol was still useful as a club

26

Short-bladed swords were less likely to get tangled in the rigging

To stop pirates boarding easily, slippery butter, dried peas and caltrops (see page 29) were put on the deck

Pumpkin Pirates

Henry Morgan 'the terrible' was an imaginative buccaneer who found a clever way out of a tight corner. After raiding a coastal city in South America, he found enemy ships blocking his exit from the harbour. So he filled one of his ships with gunpowder and put dummy pirates with pumpkin heads on board as the crew. The enemy were about to board it and imprison the 'crew', when the ship exploded, taking the enemy ship with it. The path was cleared for Morgan's escape.

Ropes kept the ships locked together

It was not easy to hit a target with a musket while the ship swayed underfoot

Iron cannon balls smashed masts and bought down sails and rigging

Pirate Weapons

Cannon fire was incredibly noisy. Shot could smash a hull to pieces, dismast the ship or destroy its rudder. Just one hit with a cannonball caused a shower of deadly splinters on deck. Chain shot (two iron balls chained together) ripped sails and cracked masts. Angrage (canvas bags of nails, nuts, bolts, and metal scraps) caused terrible wounds. Grenades and bombs were thrown down onto the decks of ships from rigging or masts. The bombs (a mixture of slow-burning rags and tar) created a smokescreen to confuse the enemy.

Pirates of the Caribbean carried so many hand weapons they looked like walking arsenals. Their aim was to frighten the enemy into submission. Their weapons included cutlasses, daggers, axes, pistols and muskets.

A pistol only fired one shot. Reloading took a precious half-minute, so pirates carried 5 or 6 loaded pistols at a time

Grenades were filled with gunpowder

Fire was a major hazard on a wooden ship

Everyone stood clear when a cannon's fuse was lit, as the force of it firing made the whole gun recoil (roll backwards)

GRUESOME TRUTH!

Pirate Elizabeth Stirland became known as 'Cutlass Liz' because of the cold-blooded ease with which she used her cutlass to cut men's throats. She was a pirate in the early 1600s and went to sea dressed as a man.

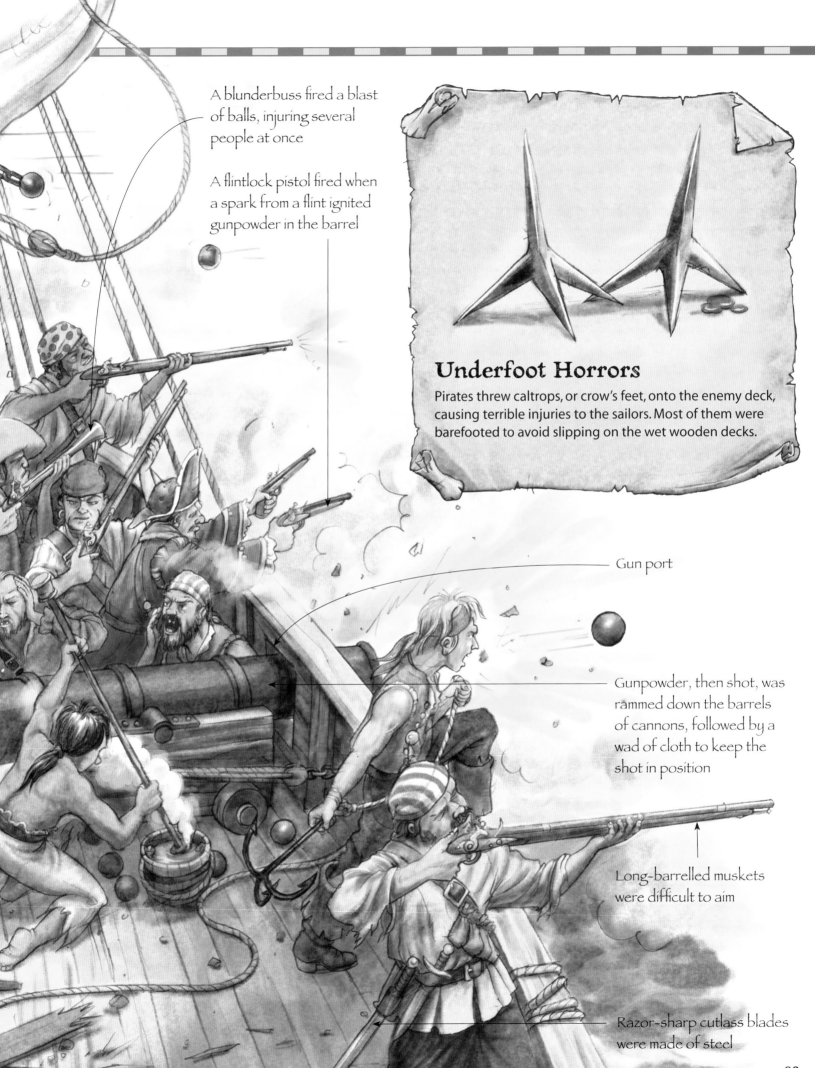

A blunderbuss fired a blast of balls, injuring several people at once

A flintlock pistol fired when a spark from a flint ignited gunpowder in the barrel

Underfoot Horrors

Pirates threw caltrops, or crow's feet, onto the enemy deck, causing terrible injuries to the sailors. Most of them were barefooted to avoid slipping on the wet wooden decks.

Gun port

Gunpowder, then shot, was rammed down the barrels of cannons, followed by a wad of cloth to keep the shot in position

Long-barrelled muskets were difficult to aim

Razor-sharp cutlass blades were made of steel

Pirate Flags

As soon as a pirate ship drew close to its prize, the captain's command rang out: "Raise the Jolly Roger!" The friendly flag that kept their villainy a secret was lowered, then the flag that filled their victims with dread was raised.

Most people think of the 'Jolly Roger' as the skull-and-crossbones. But this grisly logo was only used from about 1700. Before that, pirates flew a red banner (the 'bloody flag'), also called the *joli rouge* ('pretty red') by the French or perhaps the 'Jolly Roger' by English-speaking folk.

From 1700, pirates put all sorts of pictures on their flags. Skeletons, skulls and sharp-looking swords were especially popular. Generally, they had the same deadly message: 'Surrender, or you will die!'

Pirate flags are still a bit of a mystery because the flags themselves disintegrated years ago. However, stories and other written accounts give us an idea of who had which flag, and what they meant.

Cheers! Your Time is Nearly Up!

Black Bart had two flags – both were far from friendly. On one, a skeleton and Black Bart himself hold up an hourglass as if to say: 'Cheers!' In fact, the hourglass means: 'Your time is nearly up!'

The other flag shows Black Bart's irritation with two of his enemies: the governors of two Caribbean islands, Barbados and Martinique. The initials below each skull make his message clear: ABH means 'A Barbados Head' and AMH means 'A Martinique's Head'.

Blood-red skeleton

The sight of Edward Low's blood-red skeleton flag struck terror in the hearts of those who saw it. Low was well known for his cruelty. In 1723, he killed a Spanish crew of 53 men with his cutlass. It is also said that Low cut off and cooked the lips of one victim, and cut off the ears of another.

Swords, bones and bleeding hearts

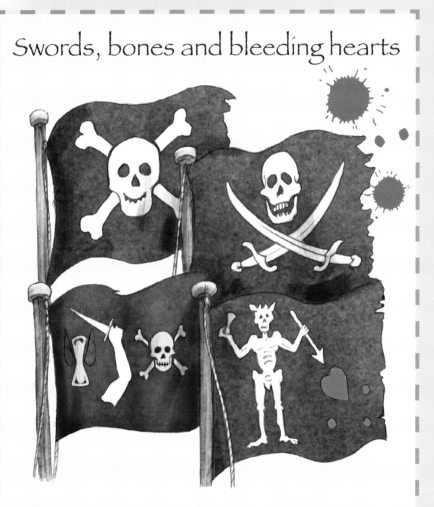

The deadly purpose behind the skull-and-crossbones flag was clear, but other flags had equally violent designs. For example, the English pirate captain, Calico Jack, replaced the bones with threatening cutlasses. North American pirate, Christopher Moody, kept the skull-and-crossbones but added a winged hourglass ('your time is flying by') and a deadly sword, so there could be no mistaking his intention. Blackbeard promoted his fearsome image with a devil-like skeleton and a bleeding heart.

Pirate Treasure

Imagine the suspense among a pirate crew, as a stolen treasure chest was smashed open. The favoured 'swag' or 'booty' was a mass of gleaming gold and silver coins. This could be transported easily, divided up among the pirate crew (by cutting coins into smaller pieces if necessary) and spent without further ado. Other highly desirable treasures included precious stones, gold and silver ingots and tableware, jewellery and ivory.

Pirates didn't turn their noses up at bulkier items, although cargo such as silks, dyes, tobacco, hides, spices and sugar were difficult to move. Also, selling them without alerting the Revenue men was a problem. The largest prize was the ship itself. Sometimes it was taken lock, stock and barrel and used as a pirate ship; otherwise, it was stripped of everything useful, such as weapons, medicines, navigation instruments, ropes, sailcloth, anchors, food – and even people, to be kept or sold as slaves (see pages 10–11).

In 1716, pirate Henry Jennings acquired 350,000 pieces of eight from just one Spanish galleon (each worth about £15 in today's money)

Mixed Results

During the Golden Age of piracy, a great many pirates acquired vast fortunes. Scores of pirate ships returned to England with as much as £1,000 to £2,000 per crewman. On one occasion every man had £4,000 (equivalent to many millions in today's money). But such treasure was not always easy to come by. Calico Jack attacked twenty ships in two years but found little of value. After attacking one schooner all he got was 50 rolls of tobacco and 9 bags of peppers!

Valuable spices from India were often difficult to sell, so might be dumped overboard

Treasures taken by Spanish invaders from Native Americans in Central and South America were in turn stolen by pirates

Jewels from all over the world: diamonds (Africa), emeralds (South America), rubies (South East Asia), pearls (Middle East)

Captain Kidd's 'Treasure Island'

Treasure was rarely buried – there was little point, as most pirates just wanted to exchange it for money to spend. Captain Kidd was an exception. Scottish born, but living in New York, William Kidd became a pirate and raided ships travelling to and from India. In 1699, he buried most of his treasure at Gardiner's Island, near Long Island, New York, just before he was arrested for piracy. He thought he could use it as ransom money. But the authorities tracked it down and Captain Kidd was hanged in 1701.

Gold from the mines in Central America was stolen in land raids, as well as from ships

Spanish silver coins (pieces of eight) were sometimes cut into pieces to share

GRUESOME TRUTH!

If pirates were caught stealing treasure from each other, a common punishment was to have their ears and nose slit.

One Spanish gold coin (doubloon) was worth two months' wages to a sailor

Pirates of the East

Fierce Chinese pirates ruled the South China Sea for hundreds of years. They hid in mangrove swamps along the coast, looting coastal towns and attacking passing Chinese and European merchant ships.

The Chinese were brilliant sailors and shipbuilders. They invented the compass and their ships were the first to have an underwater rudder and several masts. The pirates stole these ships – called junks – and armed them with cannons. Some of the most powerful pirates had enormous fleets. In the 1600s, Ching-Chi-Ling terrorised the South China Sea coast with a fleet of over a thousand junks and well-organised crews armed with muskets and pistols.

The Chinese pirate leaders enjoyed their power until the mid-1800s when the British and Chinese navies proved too much of a match. The British had by then developed speedy paddle steamers, while the junks still had bamboo sails that caught fire easily. It wasn't long before many of the Chinese pirate fleets had gone up in flames.

A Pirate Queen

When the feared pirate leader Ching Yih was killed in 1807, his wife Ching Shih took over. She was the merciless leader of crews totalling 80,000 male and female pirates. Anyone who stole from her or from another crew member was beheaded. For three years, her vast fleet of 1,800 ships terrorised the coastal waters of China, raiding other pirate ships as well as cargo ships and villages. She nearly brought all trade around China to a halt.

In 1810, her power was weakened by arguments between some of her captains. Rather than continue with a less powerful fleet, Ching Shih gave herself up to the authorities and was granted a pardon. Ching Shih then disappeared and it was rumoured that she had become a smuggler.

Wei-wei (mizzen mast)

Three masts with square sails

The rudder could be winched up or down according to the depth of the water

Pirates armed their junks with 10 to 15 cannons

The crew slept in the cramped hold, or out on deck

The cabin, where the captain and his family lived

Chung-ta-wei
(main mast)

Sails made of
bamboo matting

T'on-wei
(port fore mast)

Jolly Junks

In spite of the horrors they carried, pirate junks must have looked quite eye-catching. Many were painted in bright colours and, as well as eyes, there were paintings on their stern to bring good luck and riches.

GRUESOME
TRUTH!

For hand-to-hand combat, Chinese pirates used a heavy sword, called a two-handed hacker. It could cut off a head in one swipe.

China

Hong Kong

Pacific Ocean

South China
Sea

Pirates attacked the coastal towns of China and South East Asia, as well as merchant ships.

Eyes were carved and painted on the bow. The sailors believed they helped the boat to 'see' its way

Pirate Cruelty

You might think it was the custom for pirate captains to make their prisoners 'walk the plank' and so fall into the sea and drown. In fact, although there is one account of Black Bart making people walk the plank, there is no evidence that this ever happened. As in the Royal Navy, a common punishment was keelhauling. The victim was tied to a rope strung underneath the ship, and then pulled under the water beneath the keel (bottom of the ship) and up the other side. If the victim survived the dipping, he was still likely to die from the wounds caused by the rough shells stuck to the bottom of the ship. Traitors and deserters were marooned – left on an island with a pistol, some gunpowder, ammunition and one or two days' supply of water. They were unlikely to survive.

Eager to encourage a powerful, merciless image, pirates often chose gruesome methods of torture and murder: Chinese pirates were said to nail their victims to the deck; a crew led by Dutch pirate, Dirk Chivers, sewed up the lips of a prisoner to keep him quiet; Edward Low left a ship's cook to die in a burning ship, saying he was a 'greasy fellow who would fry well'.

Some stories of pirates on the South China seas mention the punishment of 'walking the plank', but there is no proof

Laying out a plank took effort – it would have been easier just to throw a man overboard

The punishment became well known after appearing in the novel *Peter Pan*, in which Captain Hook sent Wendy along the plank

Cat o' nine tails

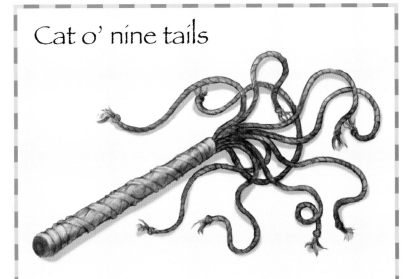

Flogging was the commonest form of punishment on pirate and Royal Navy ships. It was often done with a whip called a 'cat o' nine tails'. Each of the nine lengths of rope was knotted then covered in tar. Hooks were sometimes added to the ends. If the captain didn't particularly want the victim to die, he ordered thirty-nine strokes, as forty were thought to kill a man.

Pirate Rules

Crew members were flogged (or worse) if they broke a rule. Every pirate ship had its own rules (Code of Conduct), and any newcomer had to swear to obey them. Black Bart's rules included:

- None shall play games for money with dice or cards.
- Lights and candles shall be put out at 8 o'clock. Any crew that wants to drink after that hour shall sit on the open deck without lights.
- Any man bringing a woman on board in disguise shall suffer death.
- Each man shall keep his cutlass and pistols at all times clean and ready for action.
- Anyone who deserts the ship in time of battle shall be punished by death or marooning.
- No man shall leave until each crew member has a share of 1,000 pieces of eight.
- None shall strike another on board ship, but any quarrels will be ended on shore in a duel with pistols. If both miss their aim, they will fight with cutlasses. The first to draw blood will be declared the winner.

Pirate Punishments

If caught, pirates could often obtain a pardon by paying a ransom. Privateers were usually only imprisoned, but this was seen as similar to a death sentence as many inmates died in dirty, overcrowded and disease-ridden gaols.

In England, pirates such as Captain Kidd (see below) were hung at low tide on the bank of the River Thames in London. After the execution, the body was usually left to be covered by three high tides. Then, it was taken away for dissection by surgeons or to be buried in an unmarked grave. In America, hanging was also the common sentence for piracy. Stede Bonnet was hung in 1718 in the port of Charleston, along with his 28 crew members.

Elsewhere in the world, the death sentence was carried out in other ways. For example, Chang Jiang, a river pirate, was beheaded – as were hundreds of other Chinese pirates in the 1800s.

English pirates were hanged at Execution Dock, in London

Hundreds of people turned out to watch the executions

Captain Kidd denied piracy at his trial, saying his crew made him agree to attack two merchant ships

The pirate was brought from prison in a cart

The Admiralty Marshal carried a silver oar (a symbol of his authority)

GRUESOME TRUTH!
After Blackbeard had been killed, his head was removed and stuck on the bow of his killer's ship as a trophy.

It took two attempts to hang Captain Kidd – the first rope broke

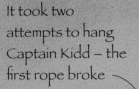

Up to his neck

In the mid 1500s, Sir Harry Stradling was sailing to his castle in south Wales, when he was captured by French pirate Colyn Dolphyn. Sir Harry had to sell several manor houses to raise the money for his release.

Two years later, Sir Harry heard that Colyn was in Welsh waters again, so he prepared an attack. Colyn was captured, tried and sentenced to be buried up to his neck in sand on a beach near Sir Harry's castle.

Captain Kidd's Sticky End

In 1701, after a year in prison, Captain Kidd was hung for murder and piracy. To warn people not to follow in his footsteps, Kidd's corpse was dipped in tar and put in an iron cage. It was hung at Tilbury Fort, on the coast of England, where it remained for several years.

The World of Pirates

Pirates were attracted to busy trade routes, like bees to honey. During the Golden Age, many pirates and privateers toured the world, sailing from one trading route to another on what became known as the 'Pirate Round'. After gathering a crew in North America, they headed for the Caribbean and the Spanish ships that were loaded with gold and silver. Next, they went to Africa to raid the Guinea coast and slave traders. Many pirates continued to the Arabian Sea, following the trade routes between Europe and the Far East. Merchant ships belonging to the British East India Company were a popular target.

In the Indian Ocean and South China Sea there were many local pirates. The Malacca Strait, for example, was perhaps the most dangerous stretch of water in the world. The Strait's swamps made perfect hiding places for local pirates. Taken by surprise, merchant ships had little chance to escape in the narrow waters.

NORTH AMERICA

Atlantic Ocean

Pacific Ocean

BAHAMAS

HISPANIOLA

The Spanish Main

Beautifully-crafted Aztec jewellery was melted down by the Spanish so that it was easier to store on ships

Aztec gold treasure

Gold and silver pieces of eight

SOUTH AMERICA

Inca gold jewellery and emeralds

The Spanish minted coins from the gold and silver they gathered in South America. Many of the coins were sent back to Spain, some of which ended up in pirates' pockets

Cape Horn

Key

Pirates		Privateers	
Pirate Round			
Barbary corsairs' ship		Spanish treasure ships	
Vikings		Chinese pirates	

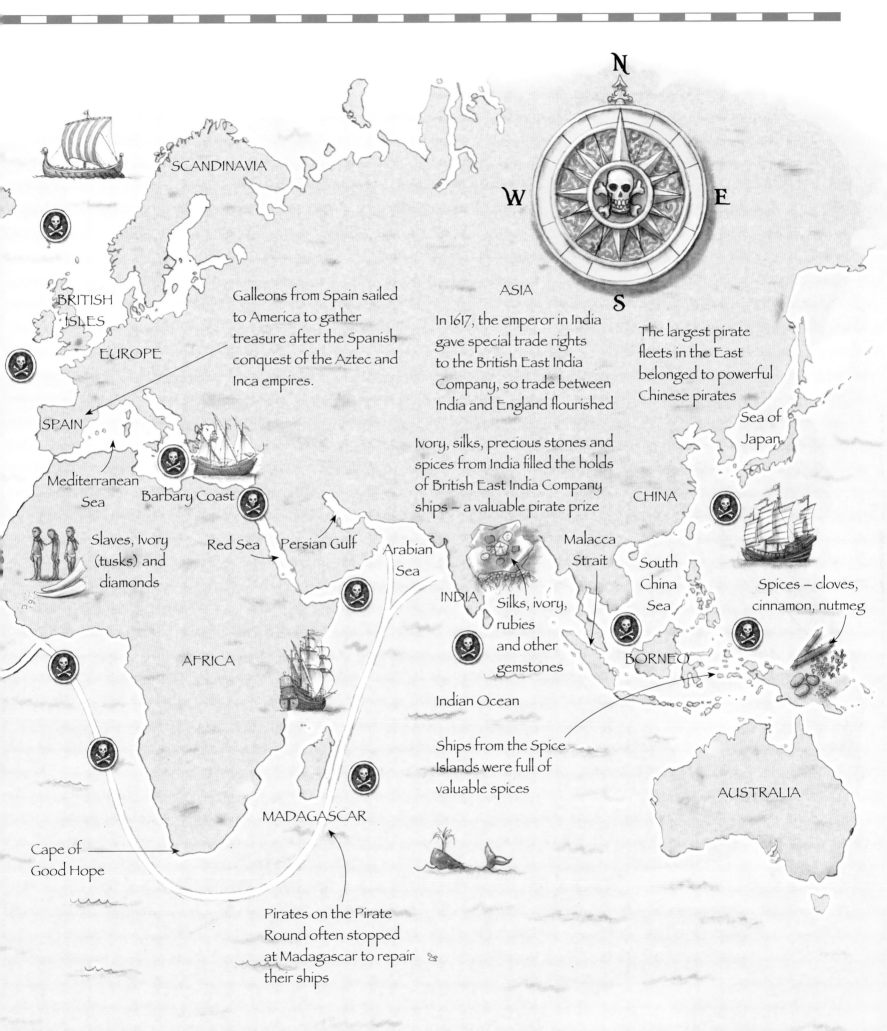

SCANDINAVIA

ASIA

N

W E

S

BRITISH
ISLES

EUROPE

Galleons from Spain sailed
to America to gather
treasure after the Spanish
conquest of the Aztec and
Inca empires.

In 1617, the emperor in India
gave special trade rights
to the British East India
Company, so trade between
India and England flourished

The largest pirate
fleets in the East
belonged to powerful
Chinese pirates

SPAIN

Sea of
Japan

Mediterranean
Sea

Barbary Coast

Ivory, silks, precious stones and
spices from India filled the holds
of British East India Company
ships – a valuable pirate prize

CHINA

Slaves, Ivory
(tusks) and
diamonds

Red Sea

Persian Gulf

Arabian
Sea

Malacca
Strait

South
China
Sea

Spices – cloves,
cinnamon, nutmeg

INDIA

Silks, ivory,
rubies
and other
gemstones

AFRICA

Indian Ocean

BORNEO

Ships from the Spice
Islands were full of
valuable spices

AUSTRALIA

Cape of
Good Hope

MADAGASCAR

Pirates on the Pirate
Round often stopped
at Madagascar to repair
their ships

Pirate Timeline

c. 500BC

Ancient Greek pirates regularly attack ships sailing near the Aegean islands in the Mediterranean Sea.

75BC

Pirates from ancient Rome kidnap Julius Caesar.

67BC

Roman General, Pompey the Great, leads a fleet to defeat pirates in the Mediterranean Sea.

c.450BC

Alvilda, Princess of Gotland, attacks ships and villages along the Baltic Sea coast.

1634

Welsh buccaneer, Henry Morgan, knighted in England for his attacks on Spanish colonies in Panama.

1617

Emperor of India gives the British East India Company special trade rights. This creates another popular, flourishing trade route for pirates.

early 1600s

Most of the world's pirates are plundering ships and coastal settlements in the Caribbean Sea.

1690–1725

The 'Golden Age of Piracy'.

1603

England's King James I withdraws all letters of marque. Lawless buccaneers such as Roche Brasiliano take over from privateers in the Caribbean.

1700

Earliest record of a 'Jolly Roger' skull-and-crossbones – said to have flown on the ship of French pirate, Emanuel Wynne, in the Caribbean.

1701

Captain Kidd is hung in London for piracy. His body was tarred and put in chains as an example to others.

1717

Notorious Caribbean pirate, Blackbeard, acquires his own ship, the *Queen Anne's Revenge*

1718

Blackbeard is pursued and killed by Royal Navy Lieutenant Robert Maynard and his crew.

2007

The International Maritime Bureau reports that pirates attacked 263 ships during 2007. Piracy is still seen as a problem, especially in waters along the coasts of Indonesia, Nigeria, Somalia and Brazil.

2003

Release of the film *Pirates of the Caribbean: The Curse of the Black Pearl*, the first in a popular series of pirate adventure films starring Johnny Depp. *Pirates of the Caribbean: At World's End* took a total of more than 200 million US dollars at box offices worldwide.

789

Vikings begin to attack people living along the coasts of the British Isles.

1217

Eustace the monk, who gave up a church job in Flanders for a life at sea as a pirate, is beheaded.

1243

Henry III, an English king, issues one of the first letters of marque, giving captains the legal right to plunder other ships and steal their cargo.

c. 1470

Birth of the Barbarossa brothers, who grew to become the most feared of the Barbary corsairs.

1570

Francis Drake, privateer and explorer, sets off on his first voyage of privateering.

1581

Francis Drake is knighted by Queen Elizabeth.

1722

Black Bart is killed by grapeshot from a cannon fired from an English warship.

1720

Anne Bonny and Mary Read are taken prisoner, along with their colleague, Calico Jack Rackham.

1523

Piracy in the Caribbean starts to increase.

1530

Christian knights establish a base in Malta and become known as the Knights of Malta.

1807

Chinese pirate Ching Yih is killed and his wife Ching Shih takes control of his ships and crews. Her fleet of junks soon controls all trade routes around China.

1816

British and Dutch ships bombard Algiers in North Africa to drive out the Barbary corsairs.

1883

The novel, *Treasure Island,* by Robert Louis Stevenson is published.

1500–1800

Corsairs paid by Christians and Muslims attack each other's ships in the Mediterranean Sea.

1819

First steamship crosses the Atlantic Ocean.

1849

The last major Chinese pirate fleet is destroyed by the British Navy.

1856

Britain, France and Russia sign an agreement abolishing privateering.

1911

The novel, *Peter Pan and Wendy*, is published. It features a classic pirate leader called Captain Hook.

1860s

Sadie 'the Goat' raids ships in the Hudson River, New York.

1850

Unable to compete with steamships, only a few pirates are left around the world.

Glossary

Aztecs – the Aztecs were Native American people who lived in northern Mexico at the time of the Spanish conquest in the early 1500s. The Spanish took Aztec gold and jewellery and shipped it back to Europe

Barbary coast – the Mediterranean coast of North Africa

bow – the front part of a ship

buccaneers – the pirates who lived on islands in the Caribbean in the 1600s. They plundered Spanish treasure ships and settlements in Central America and the Caribbean

calico – a cloth made of cotton

cannon – a large gun on wheels

cat o' nine tails – a whip with nine lengths of rope, often used to punish crew members who broke the ship's rules

colony – a country ruled by another country, or a place where people from abroad have settled

compensation – money sometimes paid to pirate crew members for an injury

corsair – a pirate or privateer in the Mediterranean Sea. The Barbary and Christian corsairs attacked each other's ships and settlements for many years. 'Corsair' is also used to describe the type of ship corsairs sailed in.

crow's nest – a lookout platform near the top of a ship's mast

cutlass – a short, broad-bladed sword first used by buccaneers. It was similar to their hunting knives

deck – a platform made of planks, which stretches across the full width of a ship

doubloons – Spanish gold coins

filibuster – a French buccaneer

fire-ship – a ship that is loaded with gunpowder, set alight and steered towards enemy ships

flintlock pistol – a pistol containing gunpowder and a flint. A spark from the flint ignites the gunpowder

galleon – large wooden sailing ship with three or more masts, commonly used as treasure ships and warships from 1500 to 1800

galley – a large ship propelled by oars; a ship's kitchen

The bow, or prow, of a ship

A buccaneer settlement

A cat o' nine tails caused terrible injuries

A seriously injured, but well-compensated, pirate

The crow's nest

A sharp cutlass could cut through skin and bone

Fire-ships filled with gunpowder were sometimes called 'hell-burners'

Pistols could only be fired once before reloading, but could also be used as clubs

Galleons were warships that carried cargo

gallows – a wooden frame from which pirates and other criminals were hung by the neck until they died

gunport – an opening in the side of a ship through which a cannon can be fired

hull – the frame or outer body of a ship

Inca – the Inca people were native American people who had an Empire in Chile, South America, at the time of the Spanish conquest in the early 1500s. Inca gold and silver was often amongst the treasure on Spanish ships that were travelling back to Europe from the Spanish Main

Jolly Roger – a pirate flag showing a skull-and-crossbones

junk – a wooden sailing ship often used by merchants and pirates in the seas of China and the Far East

kidnap – take a person away and keep them imprisoned until a ransom is paid

letter of marque – a licence allowing privateers to plunder other ships

longship – a long, narrow ship used by the Vikings

musket – a long-barrelled gun that is similar to a rifle

mutiny – when a crew mutinies it refuses to follow orders from the captain of the ship

pieces of eight – Spanish silver coins

privateer – a seaman who is legally allowed to plunder other ships. The privateer kept a share of the stolen goods, but had to give most to his employer

ransom – a payment that is demanded by kidnappers in return for the release of the person they have kidnapped

rigging – ropes that help support the masts and sails on a ship. Sailors climb the rigging to reach the sails and the crow's nest

slave – a person who is owned by someone else, and who is made to serve their owner or work for them without payment. Slaves from Africa were sold in America and so were seen by some pirates as valuable 'cargo'

sloop – a small sailing vessel with one mast

Spanish Main – the parts of Central and South America that were once ruled by Spain; also the name given to the Caribbean Sea and its islands.

stern – the rear part of a ship

Pirate slang for hanging was 'dancing the hempen jig'

The oldest junks had sails made of reeds or straw

Viking longships were powered by sail and oars

Muskets had a longer range than pistols

Sir Francis Drake, a famous English privateer

The boatswain (bo'sun) was in charge of the ship's rigging

Sloops were popular pirate ships

The rudder, at the stern of a ship, is used for steering

45

Index